The Erotic Light of Gardens

To : Irving   House

From: Jon Matteson
        &
    Christine McNeill-Matteson

Other books by Bin Ramke

The Language Student
White Monkeys
The Difference between Night and Day

Bin Ramke
The Erotic Light of Gardens

Wesleyan University Press
Middletown, Connecticut

for Linda and Nicolas

Some of these poems previously appeared in *The American Voice,
The Antioch Review, Bloomsbury Review, Boulevard, Crazyhorse, The
Denver Quarterly, Indiana Review, Mississippi Review, New American
Poets of the 80's, The Ohio Review, Pequod, Ploughshares, Shenan-
doah,* and *The Southern Review.* "Arcade: The Search for a Suf-
ficient Landscape" and "The Poor Miller's Beautiful Daughter"
were printed in *The American Poetry Review;* "Life Raft" in *The
Georgia Review;* "One View of the Wide, Wide World" in *Poetry.*

The excerpt from "Word" from *Lost Body,* by Aimé Césaire, trans-
lated by Clayton Eshleman and Annette Smith, Copyright ©
1983 by The Regents of the University of California, is reprinted
by permission of George Braziller, Inc. The excerpt from "The
Auroras of Autumn" from *The Collected Poems of Wallace Stevens,*
by Wallace Stevens, Copyright © 1954 by Wallace Stevens, is
reprinted by permission of Alfred A. Knopf, Inc.

All inquiries and permissions requests should be addressed to
University Press of New England, Hanover, New Hampshire
03755.

Library of Congress Cataloging-in-Publication Data
Ramke, Bin, 1947–
    The erotic light of gardens.

    (Wesleyan poetry)
    I. Title. II. Series.
PS3568.A446E7 1989   811'.54   88-28070
ISBN 0-8195-2171-X
ISBN 0-8195-1174-9 (pbk.)

Manufactured in the United States of America

5   4   3   2

Wesleyan Poetry

Contents

The Erotic Light of Gardens

This is where the serpent lives, the bodiless.

—Wallace Stevens

Something to Say

So where is there but the body to live?
Many have searched. The young seem to like it,
slitting their wrists in joy then languishing
long afternoons in the melting heat of love.
Even you and I, in that city of damp and delicate
air, we too spent an afternoon or two of spending.

There is no place else to live, but we mustn't
say so. There is nothing left, after the mind goes
and the spirit reveals itself for its own
thin soup of despair; refuge and reconciliation
and the lingering doubt when the tendons strain
against the weight of the head, the tendency
of each part to go its own way, of the hands to shake
palmate and practical, the toes to catch on hosiery
while teeth wear themselves to powder.

There are children, of course, who watch the wind
one afternoon, the leaves turning graceful
in some handy tree. Watch the face of some
child laughing under there, and think
of your mother back home, your father dead,
all your brothers busy with their lives, no one
thinking about what the child must do with a body
wrapped around him like blankets from firemen
after disaster some winter night:

it's why we invented language. The gallop
of the tongue across sharp teeth, the exotic
dance in there of flesh and bone and breath.
There's nothing like talking to take it all away,

all the body's ailments, its little pains
and purple bruises, its criminal tendencies.
Words filter from the skin, and sweat pours
defensively down from the brow and we eat our bread,
and all this time we thought it was sex
that saved us, we thought we were thrown out
for pleasure, and really, all along,
pain was its own reward.

The Botanical Garden

1. Fig

By your contempt shall you know him,
his laughable lawn strewn like history
with trash—smashed things saved to no purpose.

But behind his dark dilapidation of a home
children of the neighborhood threw stones
from a line of trees, a grove of figs

thick and luxuriant in pubic splendor,
public display little understood but known
to be dangerously native. The children

and birds feasted there for two weeks
each summer, the curious ingrown fruit
flagrant in their hands and beaks.

The slovenly owner of that line of trees
had pulled the leaves like curtains aside to see.

2. Snow

My mother stands at the window to stop
the dark seeping through, the sun going
despite her plea. Her shared bed and life

colder than ever, and she herself older than she'd ever
dreamed of being, back when she took the fastest shorthand
in all of Louisiana that one year in high school.

She was beautiful as the pictures showed,
or so her sisters told us. And her children
recall their father doing shift-work, leaving

led by his own shadow down the steps to work,
the weak kitchen light glinting from his hard hat.
His lunch clutched like a salvaged secret—

you should know how I hated him, his hands,
his habits, his foolish, failing plans.

3. *Nymphaea odorata*
This afternoon I with my little family walk
the frozen paths of the Gardens, the dark odors
of the drained ponds a faint ferocity

against the snow. Those ponds only months ago
fully afloat with various forms of water lily,
the languid gigantic leaves of which, monstrous

in their way, supported the weight of trash
and tin cans tossed by the curious crowds:
I doubt any malice intended, just the awe

of the ignorant. There rose above them the rose
and gold and white of blossoms, bubbles
bursting of sepal and stem that did not belong,

with nothing to do with themselves out of place,
the smell of defeat already rising.

Calculating Paradise

(Set Theory)

Former children feel such memories often,
the days when they lived at home
and watched rabbits in the evening, watched
the long shadows lope
across the lawn to the kitchen garden.
And deer, tentative as happiness, fed
on the domestic at every opportunity.

Few of you will recall the old cults
of childhood, the love of the Virgin,
lovely woman in blue who helped with homework
then kissed good night so no child slept hungry.
Longtemps, je me suis couché de bonne heure.

(Point-set Topology)

It is, like physical beauty, skin deep,
like the components of culture and curiosity
a matter of surface, a world where a man
is a doughnut, for all impractical purposes.
Theory is the last resort of the cynical.

For instance, a daughter has a boyfriend whom
her father hates, a father's favorite passion.
She opens her window every evening
to make the simple journey for love
to a streetlight at an intersection.
Some fun. The family gathered around the coffee table
assumes the silence from her room is her normal sulk.

(Tarski's Theory of Truth)

Consider, for instance, the idea of the Noble,
which is to say the theory of isolation.
When my sister talked to me of her pregnancy
it was in the language of a child, naturally.
Later, a mother herself, she hoarded those words
we had all forgotten, we few who were furtive children.

Later in the garden all eat fruit and talk.
Someone invents a word, like *geomorphology*.
Nobility, too, means learning to live alone.
The shadows lengthen across the lawn, the deer
return to the foothills, and the yellow interiors
line up all across the horizon. The City.

This is the history of civilization, or of language,
or, in other words, some of us miss each other
and talk about it long into the night, hoping.

Cinema Verité

So much I thought was only personal, like poetry,
like caring nothing for Caillebotte the man,
like arriving in Chicago by bus one gray morning
and having no place to go, going to the Art Institute
and the rain outside became nothing
next to the glorious gray of Paris, life-size.
The artist dead and all my life, I thought,
I've liked right things for wrong reasons.

My sojourn among meticulous dreams
continued. One summer I spent among smart children
taking lessons and abuse from the famous mathematician
who taught old words new: *point, line, between.*
And the long nights of teaching each other other words,
our fortunate failures. And the furious wind
blew down from time to time among us, hurricanes
which turned live oaks inside out like little minds,
mine, for instance, finding its fervent mode.

Remember that you, too, could live where men spit
while watching you and your mother pass.
That you want her for yourself alone.
Remember that those men are tall as God at such moments,
more mean. So walk among them, the afternoon cooling
within its limits, the mosquitoes taking
equally from black and white, true and false.

But there was a peninsula of time I lived on
when our family poverty left me
the couch to sleep on, the great clock
ticking terror through the night. Who can love
through his childhood insomnia? Only rain
could save me—those blessed gray
nights of noise, when sleep, like Ali Baba's
quartered brother, was sewn back together.

The Attempt to Write the Last Poem of His Life

Rimbaud did it, gave it up, like cigarettes,
and went on with the rest of his life.
I'll write a novel. I'll make a movie.
I'll sing in a rock-and-roll band.
I'll make end tables in my basement
and late at night my wife will call down
that she is going to bed. I will follow
in an hour or so and watch her sleep,
me sitting on the edge of the bed
on the edge of sleep, still excluded
from her dreams as from my own.
I'll have heart attacks. I'll have gray hair.
I'll have a son in my dotage.
We'll blow bubbles in the bathtub,
glistening spheres rising.
We'll play with his boats and washrags.
Then I'll clean his secret parts.
A daughter would do, but a boy like his father
adds symmetry: while he fumbles with toothbrush
I'll dry his legs, his feet which turn inward
from the closeness of the womb, of the wounds
of Oedipus. Otherwise we shall be
together perfectly fragile.

Harvard Classics 16, *The Thousand and One Nights*

Praise be to god . . . who hath raised the heavens
without pillars, and spread out the earth as a bed

1

The lives of former generations are a lesson to posterity.
The lives of the dead serve none of their own purposes.
That a man may review the remarkable events which have
  happened,
that someone learn something and be admonished, or at least
  amazed,
consider the history of people of preceding ages
and be restrained:

As if the telling of tales could save lives and virginity
and teach that nobility lies in complexity,
since it was to Complexity that Shahrazad prayed
while her sister Dunyzad served only the gods
Complication and Confusion.

The color of flesh is always shocking;
the veil slipped through no one's fault
aside to reveal the searing light of skin
or the horrifying glimpse in the mirror after your bath
and the dreadful fit of that skin or,
perhaps, for the lucky, the sudden lust.

So a woman lay in his bed and told stories all night
which is the same as the astronomer in his celibacy
asking the only questions worth asking,
those with no end of answers,
or at least none before sunrise.

2

What lacks passion lasts. In my own childhood
I told myself stories long into the night;
later they became erotic, and full of other
heroics than violence. I climbed the trees
whose scent and fallen needles and touch
of scaling bark could take the skin off.
Sometimes a seed fell, a brown wing broken
from among the sharp edges of the cone
(curious geometry, those fruit) twisting
in sunlight frightening as bad dreams.

I played soldier among the trees
killing quite adroitly quaint masses
of enemy—plenty to choose in the fifties,
Germans, Japanese, Koreans, the faint
remaining trace of Indians.
The lives of former generations
are a lesson to posterity.

But war well made by boys becomes
a further innocence, a pastoral procession
from a distance, like sheep grazing
beneath the cedars of a far hill,
a simple oriental pleasure like Lebanon,
and women will tell stories in the night
without end; or else I slept through it all,
perhaps lived better than I knew or loved.

3

So the child volunteered her flesh
and life to save, perhaps, the virgins
of the tribe, she the daughter of the Vizier's
complicity—and was he evil? or the king
himself a moral monster? The books don't say,
only that he killed them, out of fear
of repetition, his sultry modern mania
for the original, for verse without reverse.

There followed a thousand further versions.
There followed the consideration of histories
of preceding ages, and the contemplation
of the woman's flesh, the veil and flimsy fabric,
that he might be constrained
spread out as he was on this earth like a bed.

The Future of Supplication

A version of the modern mind: long drives,
flat landscapes, trees close up (the present) or far
against the horizon (the past) and fences strung
tight as the future, middle distance. The effect
of distance on the slow movement of landscape
past the traveler, this variorum of the present:
the family on long trips to the country,
to grandfather's famous farm
where they are only afraid of the weather.

A box turtle crossed in its creeping way the lawn
the evening we arrived, and the children followed
as if listening to his ancient whistle, his horn,
his happiness. Truly he was ugly,
yet loved are the turtles for their slow travel
in spite of the spasms of urgency they inspire.

And in the sun of kitchen garden the lizard lazes:
if the lizard were small enough
he might become a pet; large enough
to make a meal, he becomes malicious,
an Old Testament presence in the mind of modern man;

of the song of birds the *Britannica* said:
The surplus of the general metabolism
comes out—to use homely words—in unwonted functions
such as dancing, posing, spreading of feathers
and giving voice;

is this the retreat into the pastoral,
singing birds, scintillant lizards, and the view
across the lawn at evening on grandfather's farm?
Or merely fondness for fair weather?

Later in life, on longer trips, I learned the sadness
of the luggage carousel, the scuffed evidence
for all to see (such nakedness), the tattered tickets,
the mounting urgency: fear of lost luggage,
fear of weather, fear of waiting.

Remember that the serpent was no traveler,
had no such hope for habilitation.
He slithers beneath our bruising foot,
tiny purity of the present tense,
and breaks history into parts like the past
(the head) and the future (the tail)
and no one can tell the difference by looking.
He slithers beneath our bruising foot
and smiles a simple entry into worlds
so like our own we hate him:
he can't help lisping, he has no hands
to hold us back, he lives for a future
of supplication, as if the fallen world depended
upon our slender sufferings.

Life Raft

Once there was a difference
between pain and desire. The world
was not safe: ships sank, fathers
sacrificed sons to gods, and mothers
abandoned whole households, children
trussed and tossed into closets
dark as the undiscovered psyche.

And there were dangerous men who believed
that art, say, "Raft of the Medusa,"
was compensation for events, say,
the falling of hungry men upon
the flesh of the dead on
that famously fragile craft.

The world's necessary nourishment
will be provided: there are needs
greater than accuracy. Géricault
gathered heads from the guillotines
for study; little piles all over
the studio floor. And had brought
to him limbs from the hospitals
of Paris, amputations for study,
little piles of flesh:

there are several ways to suffer
not all of which are art.

As his usual practice meant sketching
until the paper darkened like evening

wracked with lines, he would trace
the best parts onto fresh paper
and go again—hundreds of versions
piggybacked of some twisted leg or two.

True, he was once famous for horses,
lively and lithe and vegetarian.
And at his own end, hospitalized,
he had no model but his own hand
to draw—how like the man of passion,
this recourse to one's own hollow palm,
whatever one's art or eros.

Nevertheless, after hundreds of studies
leading to the final painting, none
of those cannibal themes remained;
but what does any art consume
if not its own and maker's flesh?

Summary on the Coast

The basis of boredom is luck
when life without coaxing
sings you to sleep

Her eyes, and that knife-edged mouth, and she
slipped into the constant edge of water
waving like a flag in the morning water
rippling around her casual body until
she pushed off in a breaststroke pushing
reflected pennants of trees in front of her.
The boys watched from beneath their brooding.

The semen smell of pool, the chlorine,
the stain of cigarettes dropped on tile:
at night they would climb the chain link fence
to sit and smoke and then swim in moonlight,
their moon-streaked sheets in the apartments
empty, cold beds until morning.

She was there every morning, dripping already
when you arrived, flimsy in her cream suit
pulling already at the fabric, rearranging her breasts
and slipping her thumbs into the elastic
creasing her flesh, the snap and slap
of her bare feet passing you where you lay.

But to sit by a window reading
was life, too, when the air
turned solid with gelid desire.
At night there was distant lightning

and the rain thickened into translucent sheets
on three screened sides of the porch.
Thunder off the coast, east of Savannah,
filled the crevices of clouds,
surf and storm growling low as a future.

Figure in Landscape

The air was full of summer
and boys hurried to leave their sisters behind
as rudely as possible. Typical of home,
the helpful enmities of light and shade,
like the chiaroscuro on velvet
in those powerful paintings of famous saviors:
art is the mere manipulation of memory, after all.

It was a typical home, and the helpful
enmities of light and dark helped
fill the dutiful days of the wife,
the sleepy ignorance of the husband,
and the vigilant white-stoned fears of the children:
(consider the story of dark will versus lively intent,
the story of pathos and simple pleasure
derived from small events in a small town
several miles inland, full of mosquitoes
and rain, like afternoon television.

The story includes such scenes
as the changing line of lights,
the traffic lights on a Sunday evening
reflected in the rainy streets,
and other emblems of despair).
But since art is merely manipulation
after all, she watches her husband
at three in the morning sleeping,

she, having been abandoned by brothers,
a mother and a father, the System,
left alone with herself and her self,

her simple, memorable self, in the night
knows there is nothing to do but remember
and feel the flesh of one's own thigh
and wonder whether it is disease
made you what you are, or else

you take a warm bath and have a drink.
If you remember Art you remember men
watching women bathe,
Jean-Auguste-Dominique Ingres,
for instance, and the forty-eight years
between his single, torque-driven bather,
her broad back, and the later Turkish bath
of many women as if through a keyhole.
Or Delacroix, those Turkish women bathed
in the woods, or Chassériau,
whose bather sleeps like Gretel,
abandoned by her brother, too,
in the woods. Or Corot, that simple man,

whose naked bather ("La Toilette," 1859)
brought her hairdresser along under the leafy
languorous larches. You can find
Spanish bathers by de la Peña,
and any number ("The Woman in the Waves,"
"Bathers," "Bather Sleeping by a Brook")
by Courbet. Even Millet's Goose Girl
has a naked left heel cooling in the pond.
Gérôme, Bazile, Degas, Gleyre, Renoir,
Puvis de Chavannes, Gauguin, Cézanne,
and Guillaume-Adolphe Bouguereau,

all these men imagined women bathing
indoors and out, even seeing
these naked bathers sleeping, open air,
closed in their own memories
for the dangerous delight of men.
But what memory does she suffer, our wife,
bathing at three A.M., following her shining
way back into the dark wood?

The breast which emerged in sunlight
curves like limestone beneath her sleeplessness.
Driftings of forgetfulness descend
like shells of small animals to fit
the shape of ocean floor, or the vitreous
shape of the bathtub, white and domestic.

One View of the Wide, Wide World

He saw the green hills.
He saw the river.
And far, far away
he saw the blue sea.
     —*E. H. Minarik*

1

A bear climbs down
a tree overlooking the sufficient world:
the tops of trees, his own house, his mother bear.
And there is what might be a shepherd
in the drawing by Maurice Sendak, and a boat
tacking carefully into my son's memory, too.

Rhythm is random, *felix culpa* tall in the ear,
as when all carpenters on the roof
accidentally end their day's work with the first
four notes of Beethoven's Fifth Symphony—
I have heard it happen, faultless as a pearl growing.

A story comes back again, soothes the single
mind again. Or underlines the farther edge
beyond the blue sea, the black slough,
the night which surrounds his very bed,
the night which follows every bedtime story.

And thus he called to me this night
I could not sleep for the vision, the girl's arm
missing below the elbow, beating a tinny tattoo
over and over: why has medicine, like the sleep
of children, made no progress over time?

2

My mother read me a story of a bear
who climbed down from his tree and met
a little girl lost in the woods.

This was while my mother's sister hides
from my uncle, who was angry, and my father
has a gun and stands behind the door

and there is a knocking.
Later I have dinner
at my uncle and aunt's house and no one

will tell me the story of that night,
they have all forgotten, but I
remember the little girl and the bear

who had seen the world but still
held her hand and showed her the way
home by the river, where her family

lived in a tent, and birds sang.
The girl had a doll whose arm broke
when she fell from a tree at a party.

3

Grandmother who is dead smiled
in spite of her arm in a sling;
I climbed trees in her yard.
There was a river and the Gulf
of Mexico was out there beyond the river.
There is always something beyond the river.

I had an uncle who sailed the sea.
I had an uncle who farmed.
One was a forester for TVA.
Two of my uncles were blind.
I had a father and a mother.
I never met a bear, though I was
many times lost in the woods.

No Kinder Subject

She lives alone now, the short-legged mother
whose waddle through seven children's lives
left scars and scandals and some comforts.
She raises things. The city rose
around her messy as any child. She plucks
apples when it is time, carves a bed for dahlias
when the season strikes. TV for an hour, then bed.

Whatever hunger hallows her little memories,
whatever lessons linger along the hallways,
her former husband remains dead, deliriously
drowned in something like the past, the danger.
The upper Carboniferous of the late Paleozoic
was his specialty: there is no kinder subject,
no more generous passion than geology,
the wise world layered delicate as cake
toppling tyrannies with time and tiny bodies:
all gone, all going, Cretaceous—chalk it up
to experience, learn a little something.

But you should have seen, she said, *the garden*
your father made before the war, the one
along the coulee, the one with bougainvillaea
assaulting the cypress, and sweet pea covering
any loose limb or fallen trunk. It was his pride
before the children came, before the war.

And after, there was work, and learning
the meanderings of rock, the slime and slip
of whatever might mean clean treasure underground.
His old clematis climbed the rotting barn

through all, through wars and children.
One must cover the roots with a large rock
or something cooling like the grave,
then let them bloom in sunlight, bear the heat above.

When they were children they fished together
in Vermilion Bayou. They didn't know each other
for years afterward. They fished and sometimes
saw the water snakes slide scurrilous and smiling,
slide along the surface, their heads high, slim
necks digging a slight dimple in the water,
the body nearly covered. In those days
they spoke their native language, and they knew
a solemn little world, a string of slender nights.

What the Servants Thought

Day unto day uttereth speech
and night unto night showeth knowledge.
—*Psalm 19*

It takes time and it takes distance
to tell the truth or lie.
Think of this man riding home from his
necessary sinning. His headlights
a thin yellow stream against the dark.
And the remaining woman stands in the doorway
the milk bottle in one hand, her robe
close against her breast in the other.

He has no friends to speak of, or to.
Men like him keep their own faith
driving down little ways, narrower
streets where the houses are smaller,
closer packed, the potholes sharper edged,
where children know him and dogs
lick his hand.

You can see his condition in many men's lives,
the love that burns brighter for wives wronged.
Nothing attracts like despair from a married man.
Alone in strange rooms listening to plumbing
he dreams of release, of a time when the body
becomes a shadow wavering on the surface
like a flag on wind, a body beyond itself,
a body borne by force of clean intellect
haunting nothing but mind, vast and noble:
I have more than once conducted
complex affairs with women.

He has read all the women's magazines,
all the articles on living alone
or with husbands who travel, or with children
filled with their lusts and languors.
He can name their perfumes shyly smeared
with trembling small hands in the ladies' rooms,
the bottles they keep hidden
beneath the panties all week.
He knows more about lingerie than any salesman,
the sheen in moonlight; he has seen
the sad flash of cotton in the flickering
moth-glow of streetlight.

During that rainy season when he proposed
he would walk beneath dripping dogwoods
to spy on her, her apartment, the golden
incandescence of her window through mist,
and would see movement, a shadow, his heart
breaking open like a flower. But it was never
another man, and she was always home.
That terrible love he bore which she wanted
broke hearts and minds and made him mean.
All he really wanted was his own rented room
with a television for baseball and
a keeping of meticulous score.

But once when insects shivered against the lawn
and the sun glinted on darkening grass
and their glasses sat like dragonflies
on the noses of women reading books,

the boy gazed through the lozenged gazebo
to admire their hats, their long fingers.

But he never learned that foreign tongue,
and when he looked again they were gone.
Books face down on the chairs marked chapters
in which other women watched boys
play in the green evening light.

Further Delay

Reasons for travel ("if blackberries were reasons
I would give you reasons") abound in books
and business. Some of us profess to dislike it.
But our various visions bring us these seasons

together, talking in tiny groups echoing large
in the airports. It is a form of life. Good
as many. What the body accomplished it accommodates,
food and frail naps and sly sips at departure.

But these momentary manias, this falling into—love?
And why not? These falls into the liquid lives
of fellow passengers, the tiny woman there among
a small city of luggage, her life awaiting you, above

all else she is as alone as you, and wears her vivid fear.
How can you return home without her? Or consider
that small Syrian family, and the daughter delightful
in all ways you will never know, nor even overhear.

During every war of this current eternal century
the rail, bus, or air terminals have served
the domesticating functions, the civilizing project
of delay—less quickly into and out of danger surely

is something, some consolation. The moaning
of small old men, the dry cries of children
form a simple melody behind it all,
all life funneled slowly forward, slowly home.

Tarzan and the Slave Girl

Another kingdom afflicted, another chance
for pleasure (in the form, naturally, of blonde
women from the heart of Africa) to die
at the hand of duty: Lee Sholem, director,
black and white, 1950.

Duties afflict us all. Even the vexed question
of what one's duty is. Politics has a season
in this country, and another such is upon us:
our delirious duty to the movies once more,
to find new ways to see the world whole,
less hard on us all, all the extras.

Meanwhile lovely ladies wash laundry along
the foaming river, and two elephants,
mother and daughter, pass by. Cheetah, who is
a chimpanzee, rides behind. Tarzan, as European
as any, more certain of his duty, rides ahead.
There is evil in the bushes, there is a bird
mysteriously frightened. Screams from the shadows.

The inverse square law: what else diminishes
with the square of distance? If the sound
of the train shifts from blue to red, and the TV
sifts electrical snow on your one child who churns
in his sheet like a cone of cotton candy, turns
tighter in the package of himself until morning,

then it is time to consider comets. On Christmas
night, 1758, a farmer-astronomer named Palitzsch
saw it again. Mr. Halley, dead for sixteen years,

still patted the predictable hand of the nervous world
since what returns reassures, surely. What comes back
can't be all bad if there's a back to come to.
What's named is tamed. Halley's Comet. Big Bertha.
Fat Boy. And there is solace in cycles; after all,
eighty-five years is merely human. "Thou art come!
a matter of lamentation to many a mother art thou come . . .
threatening to hurl destruction on this country."

Or take Christmas itself. What returns reassures
and X marks the spot, buried treasure, a grave,
or even, this time, on the map of memory a birth:
Xmas. Even if the date, not to mention the man,
is mythical, the day builds, red in the air,
and snow, and you are driving home for the holiday.
Dark and the lights of oncoming cars slide
across the windshield, the windshield crossed
by the wipers hissing in sequence, trying
to make an X against the future, clearing the way.
Something to look forward to, goodly giving,
food for the lucky, and late languishing.
Some child born in a stable later learns to cure
blindness, to die famous in the shape of *Y*.

Still, when the last bomb falls, the finger that pushed
the famous button having already evaporated,
and the rubble is stirred a last time this late
afternoon of the war, is there a sound?
When the dewy earth has finally cleaned itself
of the last least microbe, when the lava finally
flows leisurely through the cracked crust,

then what is the sound of one hand clapping?
Pain purifies, but sometimes the whole house goes
up in flames when all you wanted was a sterile needle
to remove a splinter, another little Kingdom lost.

On Hunger as Hardest of Passions

A

The poetry of praise is political.
To praise X is to reject Y, thus
the beloved of the love poem lives
at the expense of the not-loved.
People in their bright rooms expand
through the night; through doors and
screened windows their discussions
of politics, religion, and art filter.
Among these people one tiny self
across the street seems to be turning
a page, her knees glisten under the lamp.
She might be loved. She is reading
her seed catalogues. Praise her.

B

It is sad when this man pretends he is in love
just to know how it feels, as when in school
he skipped lunch to know compassion for the children
of Bangladesh. But the world continued hungry.
The smell of flowers saves no life. So
let us praise such contentment as is known
by the starving children; they pretend there is food
which they never really wanted, after all.

C

Descending the stair at midnight, hungry,
heading for the kitchen he passed
the hyacinths simmering on the table

and suddenly understood: the issue is not
that the emperor had no clothes, nor even
that an entire kingdom could be fooled
(the gullibility of children to be dealt with
in a footnote to follow), but the issue,
he now in his midnight hunger understood,
has always to do with belief: the naked
emperor or poet reflects the clarity of vision
of The People. Such a vision could save
the silent world—all but the children,
those faithless brutes.

D

Discreet placements, long walls, mazes
Against the dangers—a garden. The long-lived
Foolishness which comes with seasons like spring
Found a weary place in this family,
Offered to help with the dishes or rake the paths.
Deciding this was no proper place for hunger,
Indiscreetly, one morning, it murdered all
Lying in their innocent beds, bulbs and all.

Plainly, what the quaint couple knew and loved was
Unusual circumstance, three-ring circuses and a way out,
Retreat in the face of fire: the last to leave the room
Please turn out the lights. This was adequate basis for
Lifetimes together, they reasoned, surely. Meanwhile
Every week someone's mother sent groceries and the
Lonely father came one afternoon with drinks
Offering a barbecue grill and a TV. Life was good,

Only, they were miserable with each other
So the years teach one nothing. Joseph Cornell
Even could live with a mother happy enough
Silent on Utopia Parkway. Who would ask for anything more?
They made a garden. First walls, concrete studded with
Red shards glittering in the sun, slender blades of green,
Indigo and gold, broken glass brilliant. Then came
Footpaths, pleasant twinings smooth but with texture
Enough to please, at least, the feet.

Redeemed rock and scrub—foolish plans, but
Otherwise it was a start. And they tiled three gazebos.
Set out osier and wattle fences. And a Troy Town centered.
Elsewhere a *manneken-pis* for fertility.

In the midst of such plentiful
Reason for joy, the jealous incidental cause,
I.e., the children, incrementally added their measure,
Sentimentally pissing into the pond.

E
Valadon, Utrillo's mother, when asked
about their famous past would find a fitting letter
to destroy, as any force of history should.

That moment in the shade of Red Mountain
when the magpie flew among us, brushed
accidentally the sleeve of that woman
who reminded me of you, and like any sordid past
disappeared into the music—the low notes,

the dark flourishes like any woman's wish
to be rid of the man, the likes of him,
that moment in Aspen at the festival.

Collect enough such moments and make a life.
Like Utrillo's mother, whose truest paintings
proved nothing to her child. But among
the mountains a museum held nine Cornell boxes,
among which a former boy gathered
to himself the dark blue room, the hush
like reverent mystery, before he returned
to the terror towering, real mountains.
"Lady on Horseback," circa 1952, for instance,
is about what happens when light lingers
all evening and there is music mirroring
and there is the occasional sound of a child
laughing at a dog during the concert.
All of us without tickets gathered on the grass
listening through the tent's booming canvas,
and the dog with the past in his teeth,
the patient child's pet, and we all heard
the dark feathers among the minor keys,
the hush of wings. And of course
there was the danger, the damage dogs do.

Compulsion as the Critical Element
in a Defined Perversion

To become acquainted with such a self as this
watching warily through the window half-
silvered by the encroaching dark—the night
only, no symbol, no vast reverberation fearsome
in far-reaching relevance—such a self as this
man trampling the late tulips and early
ferns fiddling their little heads above the loam,
was never matter of moment for her. She welcomed
only men of mere mystery, left the lust alone.

The weather alters often enough. The world
of wind and wetness suffices itself and soon
repeats. Wait for a warm day, and evening
will come. Wait for frost. It creeps
along the stems of little grasses and holds
its stiffening phallic folly long enough.
Then goes with the weather wherever.

She never thinks about it. Birds whisper
their prattle, meaningful enough.
No wonder she closes the window, the blinds.

Arcade: The Search for a Sufficient Landscape

The Pontalba Apartments in the View-Master
and the cardboard cathedral as if trapped in the dream
twenty years early, the whole a furious search
as if for a reason. Still, it's sex that spoils it, isn't it?

Jackson Square was the smallest sufficient landscape,
but that was before, and now the gates are locked
at sundown, and the smell of the river fails,
falls ever backward. Some of us lived there, though:
What shall we say who have knowledge
carried to the heart? Back then those flat façades
shone on young couples acting like lovers
or something, sitting on the bench, listening
to chimes, living on doughnuts.
There were pink roses on the iron fence
washing white in the streetlight.

Sometimes on a Sunday afternoon
a nice person owns a house of pink stone
with green lawns and little statues lining the drive.
Sometimes there are maids at the windows
shaking things in the breeze, sheets and pillows.
Sometimes those houses have gardeners
whose slim shears glisten in the sun, whose powders
and viscous liquids kill the slugs and common
little moles and dank dwellers.
But in the movies there is music for anything.

Every man matures in spite of himself,
thus deserves no credit after all. Another landscape

opened once on Ursulines Street: a convent
conveniently tended by tall nuns stooping.
Sounds of sprinklers somewhere in the air,
the smell of sanctity and rose dust, brief and golden.
Carson McCullers thought it a party to which
she had no invitation. I would have told her
how it was, taken her for walks among the herbs.

But young men have no school for love, alas,
learn what we can too late, too lingeringly,
then women wither from us like the state.
Children abuse us mightily, running off
to play in traffic along any dangerous life,
daring us to die or watch trying.

Memory Gardens, they are sometimes called,
often lovely *cimetière*, as Mallarmé would say,
Egypte ancienne—embaumements, the same forever:
Haven't we all planted a friend or two, a father
or a daughter or a distant cousin? My father's house
a mausoleum. Here the landscape means business, boy.
Here the man with the shovel is king.
(More truly today, the man with a backhoe.)
I also like the green, grassy rug they throw
over the dirt, the sweet discreet mound
rising humbly among the mourners, hands folded
at crotch level, eyes focused inward
or on the ankles of your favorite cousin.

There is sometimes a walk afterward
among arcades and hanging cascades,

along the lyric delphinia and daphne.
You talk with your scandalous cousin who lived
twelve years with a man in Brazil.
She tells you about the bougainvillaea
both pink and white. And you say
how your job keeps you indoors most of the summer:

tall in the ear, cathedral quiet and dark
in its own soothing sort of way, lingering
like the tap of the tourist's toe on terrazzo,
her memory, your cousin's presence after all
these years remains. Love, you might say,
but would she remember your visits
among the gravestones, and your vows of celibacy
and your attempts late into the nights to settle
the issue of Fermat's Last Theorem once
and for all? She sees her version
of your sad affair; you see the sordid
evenings at prayer in the cathedral, your beads
entangling, your hands shuddering into spire-
shaped wings wafting as if with incense
into the hopeless future you shared so gladly,
you who call yourself a man or a woman.

Better Late than Never

I was young once, at least, if not beautiful.
And what is beauty anyway? The light off snow
is pretty. I was young once, as young as any.
After all, she thought, to know the edge
of truth or of mountains, you need to lie or fall.

Everyone has an inner life, O careless love,
it's as simple as that. That's why they hurried
to marry before the month ended—fear of June.
She would avert her eyes from the magazines'
special issues with brides on their creamy covers.

He worked to replace her money he'd squandered.
Then came a time of last intimacy, her injections,
when once a week he'd puncture with the silken needle
her arm, her condition worse with age, her pain
made him wince and call her Dear; her alluring allergies.

From where they retired all views were distant,
nothing true or tender at hand. Mountains to the west
like pets kept for good weather or loneliness
and the need for cold to gloat upon.
They would sometimes think of history together,

of the choked passes which killed, of the grasses of summer
when water was rare and expensive as illicit love.
With the interstate smooth as needles gleaming beneath
the snow-slick peaks, they would think of pioneers
lost and together, alas, two by two, with beds as baggage.

Another edge to be cut on. She loves the little
line of houses or trees in landscapes, the thin
horizons hugely bearing the weight of drama
and of sky with its tooth of cypress or steeple.
And he, while he turned the wheel and tuned the radio,

what was on his married mind? He remembers often,
these latter days, the cousin he first loved,
her marriage to an ugly man when he lit the candles
and wore the little suit his mother made,
and he cried for her because she was only beautiful.

He remembered riding in the car from the library,
having taken a book on Freud because his cousin
was studying Freud, and such studies were forbidden
his Catholic childhood. And riding in the back seat
as his father drove he read about the fountain pen

as phallic, the ink seed of Onan spilled, and he
grew sick and felt the frisson of guilt and glory.
And she was married to an ugly man, but the world
conspires to avert its eyes, and the needle-sharp
peaks hover behind them as the little dashes of white

lines spurt out beneath their car on the highway home,
a little line like spoor marking their path, so easy
to retrace, ready made, like everyone's. So there's
no need to look, just live long, since youth is truer
than beauty, Love; long life and many children.

The Private Tour: Circle 7, Round 3

What boy doesn't, once, admire his father?
There was nothing to be known he didn't know,
that day, about water. I entered behind him
great electrical caverns where cascades like
the tropics fell cleanly to cool air
for operating rooms; I crawled with him through
boilers down, bulging with rust and power.

He taught me to titrate, and to pronounce
fine-grained words, and to think full phrases
like parts-per-million, like Erlenmeyer flask.

When a man dies he divides the world precisely
as any chemist can. Having ridden the beast
he tells his child, I will ride between you
and the tail, lest you be poisoned by it.

Es Könnte Auch Anders Sein

The inner man has no language.
—*Louis-Ferdinand Céline*

1

Only at that point did it become a little frightening.
And since the recounting of dreams requires
intense accuracy, effort inversely proportional
to the effort of dreaming itself, I tell it carefully:
A snake filled the tree next to the barn where
I milked the cow each morning before school, the barn
merely a shed, a corrugated metal skin on trembling
timbers tied with wire to lean against the wind;
the boy feared everything but snakes, despised
the cow who bullied him with her horns hurrying.
The dream snake filled the sky, filled the tree
which in turn filled the sky by the barn—
and only as it moved each scale simultaneously,
not a movement front to back but all at once the whole
a murmuring mass, only then it felt
a little frightening, and I called out.

2

The original is overbearing, overburdened,
and temporal. I am a child of translation,
the last country to love: there, the most mysterious,
lightest of realms, where no man's magisterium
subjects word to meaning except that the infinitely
malleable turns itself into The Other—*ander*;
like the milky-colored crackling skin of snake,
meaning sloughs into rocks and thorns along the way.
What is it of shapeless childhood that wins
in the end, that defeats you? That snakes back

one night into your gingerly grown-up life,
your compromise, your version of a self worth
forgiving? What snake, and what did it mean?

3
The barn hid various shames where his brothers
hid that magazine. Where he could watch,
his eye close to the metal hole, for people
coming while he dreamed over the pictures.
Not dreaming. *Imagining*, too, is wrong.
An untranslatable concept, formless, the mind of boy
desiring to descend into its slickest self,
the scales covering the eyes with that same
translucence of snake just before his molt
when the skin clouds and all he sees is light,
when all he does is swim up through milk.

4
A little man in a room labors at his desk over the poems
of the dead Italian. The little man knows many things.
The little man labors mainly at night, sleeps or stumbles
through the day, the dry and dreary. But evening
and the star (some Venus or Mars) finds him
fiddling again, filling his little pages with the words
he wished were better, fuller, more like that knot
he feels beneath the rib, the better poem, the one
he wrote as if to be read only in translation,
only in some other mother tongue, the minor note,
the glistening poem in the tree, every scale moving,
the whole a murmuring mass. Only then
it feels a little frightening, and he calls out.

Buchenwald

Like the last laugh calved by innocence
—*Aimé Césaire*

An orange butterfly trying to drink the tears
of an alligator drove the beast blinking
back to the swamp; the event means nothing
beyond itself and is random as words which mean
only their own use, for instance,
the German for *beech grove*, also subject
and title for a lovely little landscape
by Klimt, *um 1902*: useless innocence gathers
in the form of words like the children
of prostitutes accumulating the last
praxis of passion, accumulating

like clouds on the horizon. *Mon dessein
en est pris*, wrote Racine somewhere
(*Phaedra*), which is to say the design
is taken, which is perhaps, the translator
would say, to say my decision is final.
Design is not decision, nor is tragedy
random, nor is translation less than noble
in intent, whatever its traduction.
To reassemble into resemblance is something
and drives rough beasts in the manner of children
with sticks and stones into the swamp,

into the innocence of the original. The design,
the tailor says, of it is taken. You may go,
your dark suit will fit you tomorrow
and much mourning becomes us. But
we mostly mourn not people but possibilities

while the crepy skies descend most humbly
upon the day, upon the evening meal of wounded women
and mangled men who tried to talk to each other.
Their dense surrender dark as fruit
on the table, pits and seed and assorted
tangibles causing teeth to crack, teeth of the careless.

Let us bite into something solid for once
and consider the dark words—*négritude* being now
abandoned, the politics of simple sound lost,
of second world wars and third-world policies
and the exotic Francophone politics of Martinique,
for instance; the word traduced. And my own surrounding,
sometimes French-speaking, people spoke
in something passing for innocence

of *colored people* except when the needs
of anger produced *nigger* (from the French
nègre), in defense of darkness. Meanwhile
in a wood where the Brothers Grimm collected,
the smoke of a new form of fashion rose
from another oven. Save us,
Gretel cried, from the obliterating hunger,
huge and cute, of innocence. Or else just let
me and my brother go back into the forest dark
and deep, the lovely long white stems, the *Buchenwald*.

The Poor Miller's Beautiful Daughter

1

We are invited to summer evenings in the colony
in spite of the threats, the heat, and the talk
of strangers. No matter which theory the tourist
(alas for the life of leisure) used to excuse the bombs,
the view was shattered surely, the lovely coast charred
and the small delightful children discouraged
from their tender pursuits.

It is hard to believe she was killed, she
whom the archbishop liked, even quoted one Sunday
in his most benign sermon among the lilies,
among the scents and sanctities proper to his station.
In her time she was innocent, full of zeal.
But bombs no longer fall, they linger
domestic as sunsets among these islands,
slippery as postcard landscapes, thorough
as the minor household insects, the flies.

She liked the rich, didn't she; enjoyed
the way they smell and smile in good weather.
She could live among them. She talked to herself
and they listened, thinking themselves addressed,
never considering otherwise. She passed for one
of their children. She held her hope as they held
money, secretly shining like radium.

There was a time she moved among the poor
when music was visible and thick and the food
forgettable but the nights lasted forever
and secrets fell like stars for those watching

and there seemed to be an end in sight, millennial.
It was wrong of her to think that way:
it was wrong to join those clubs
which elect no officers
and collect no dues.

When the bomb went off a young priest (they said
a handsome young priest) was standing
near the door. His left arm cocked in a sort
of question mark against his hip, and a book
waving in his right hand. His soutane flapped
in the breeze of concussion when the door
shattered and the glass shivered into his back.
He would no doubt have forgiven all.
He never had any luck,
his mother later said.

The body is its own map, readable in the dark
or on the operating table, or in its own cool bath.
The hand, the pure palm, tells some small story,
sad as any ending, but you must read the whole body
to know something like a secret, like those causes
people think they die for.
Anyway, where they die is home.

2
After all, after it all, some survive.
A girl can make her own living, central
figure in her own confinement, still point
in a turning world of men. In this place

the sun never shines, and men wander avoiding
each other's eyes, placing coins in the various
machines, watching movies or live ladies
behind glass. Sometimes there are telephones
too, and sometimes she just paces like Rilke's
panther, *ist wie ein Tanz von Kraft um eine Mitte,*
in der betäubt ein großer Wille steht.
To the amazement of the law, this is not
prostitution; there is no touch, only torment.
It is a bit of art, timeless behind the trick
with lights which reflect his own face until
he pays and then her vision swims into his ken.

3
It is another in a long list of dangers,
a father's too enthusiastic presentation
of his daughter's skill. Still, one wonders
where the idea of straw into gold arose,
not to mention why the king did not suspect
the miller's household of some deceit.

Rumpelstiltskin, the only man to bear faith,
worked through three full nights:
isn't it the story of the lilies once again,
who neither sow nor reap but get the power
and the glory, not to mention a child to keep.
She who had no skill to start with, no hope
through the first night, and no honor,
never meant to keep the bargain gladly made.

The politics of innocence comes to this:
Get a good lawyer, or practice holy terror.
To scream the aisles clear, to throw a fit,
is a way to get your way, after all.
No tiny sovereign in our time has missed
this lesson. But this story's tantrum
was another act of love; a small man
who loved a child and did all that he was asked:
for this, his poor heart's body torn in two.

Cliff Dwelling

The sound of the stone falling astonished him,
then the stunning size of it, the earth,
the green mesa surrounding itself with weather.
Thunder echoed down the canyon in a way reminding
him of the culvert near what was once home
and his father's far voice echoing him
back for dinner. And lightning against the purple,
and twelve ravens exactly weaving and wafting
themselves to this place where some kind of Indian
had built its temple to the sun.

To prove an edge to this world, the sun
was setting, bright rim. But why not
(and who would see anyway) cry?
Even a stopped clock tells correct time
twice a day. He trusted himself and cried,
then crept down the ladder carefully
when the rain finally reached him, and the cold.

The sun, insolent in its languor, descended
marking millennia by minutes withdrawing
its gold glare from Anasazi walls,
the few unfallen wedged like time
into accidental cracks which is all
anyone now knows of childhood.

Hierarchy

You might establish order on this basis:
simple to complex. My grandfather driving a car
which any farm fool could keep in good repair,
my grandfather driving the DeSoto, sleek and simple,
wide and riding its springs like ocean swells,
the old ways clean and speed determined by recent ruts
or the need to wave to friends on front porches.
My grandfather's simple ethic, his bigotry, riding
like some barge on the waves. Good country people.

It can be according to movement, i.e., the snake's
unfortunate reputation derives
from his sinuous locomotion, his tendency
toward slipping lithely through grasses and herbs
or, when he aspires to higher limbs,
he sometimes falls upon the stray traveler.
Thus the happy fault of humans becomes entwined
in the firm grounding of the serpent.
Birds' bright plumage is no reason to prefer them—
the snake is sleeker, shines his magnificence
and glitters bright as any child's eye.
But the birds fly, alas, which we prefer
though they will eat the worst and warmest things of earth.

Or our willful tending to matters of size:
"David" and *La Tour Eiffel* turned silly souvenirs,
or Monticello, not to mention the man, in our pockets.
These and other examples. Or the other side of the coin,
the cunning of bonsai, the triumphant ship in the bottle,
the brilliance of postage art flashing
on the first-day cover, Trieste to Vancouver, worldwide.

And the father who remains beyond any son,
some stern Noah glimpsed in his nakedness,
his naughty genitalia forever following
the poor boy's failings. Consider that even
the ocean's grandeur resides
in nothing better than bland immensity, stupid size.

Even age itself differentiates. Within the family
we recall the wisdom or the simple-minded mess
of our parents, our potted heritage, dotty darlings.
Or the gemlike flame some new baby brings momentarily.
Geology too divides the basic steps
into the dismissible new, the reverential ancient,
like Iceland or the Rockies. Cronus killed by his sons.

Or the face of your beloved in sleep, relaxed
into all its latent ugliness. The problem of the binary,
the antihierarchical Yes and No, Male and Female,
Off and On, Good and Evil. Lying under a tree,
lying under two trees, in fact (competition
between the oak and some oriental in the park), he saw
the breeze move a limb and brutal sun expose
two birds, two hot sparks of life pouncing
on the righteous and unrighteous alike
in the dappled shade around. Sparrows unfallen.
The tree before him, smooth bark curiously ridged
as if made of bound bundles, oriental, as if
a bundle of snakes bound waving their tails as limbs.
The passing of an airplane against the wind's direction,
a small boy lurking in the shadow, lucky boy.

An old man sitting on the bench driven away
by the young couple in love, displaced in turn
by the couple with one child who was disturbed
by the group with music, et cetera.

With your eye level to the hedge you can see
all across the park, all parts receding,
the great gray gashes of water spraying like artillery,
the bicyclist floating like a lean-faced bird hurrying.

On the Eve of the Revolution

The children heard, the others kept eating.
Rain trickled through the ancient roof
Down the triangles of beams through
Electrical connections, then dripped

Off rococo teardrops of the chandelier.
Three drops had fallen into the gravy
And father had watched them splash brown
As rain does into puddled manure at the barn.

A shower of sparks then darkness. Mother
Held her knife at her still breast.
The servants moved to the cellar

To change the fuse. We finished the meal
By candlelight, watching our shadows
Mimic our movements, hand to mouth.

Elegy as Origin

1

Begin, Boy, with a thought, and once thinking
Continue to consider that there *is* a world there,
Though Nature's neither consolation nor timid toy
But is enough if sure of itself, sleek *Ding*

An sich. So go on a trip to the country, slip
Into something comforting, watch lumber lumbering
Bearish and brute of the dirt itself, alive
Along with all the little things that get their grip

While you sleep, that make you sick by morning.
Meanwhile in Paris the war continues. Your mother
Listens on the shortwave to reports of your death
By poetry, and with long, sure, purple mourning

The workers in the vineyards memorize long
Passages of your famous poem, "The Famous Boy and His
Mother." Backstage at the Opéra one of the many former
Lovers you reluctantly left rehearses a dirge, song

Of solemn fornication. The wolves listen on the steppes
For word of your fate, the stars glimmer turning
Themselves to tears, dissolving their clear
Pure tonality into torment. Death is inept

Except in extremest measure—*you'd* never seek
Such carrion comfort, but what's a boy to do who's seen
The world, Paris in particular, who milked cows
On school mornings and knew bird calls but no Greek?

The body buys its way back; the body is a walled
City, a secret garden full of snakes and apples
And has its own will and way with itself and
Its simple foolish brain-bashed languages called,

Culled easily out of itself: the body is its own
Simultaneous translation, self to self, explaining
Everything, soothing past and present into a pause
Which it labels "self" and carves into the bone.

2
Your only triumphs were musical, like
Cliburn, not Napoleon, in Russia.
What any army does is less, more long-
suffering even when it fails defeat.

The absurd obligatory coughing of the audience
during every pause, the festival of phlegm
at every concert—how you hated the sounds
of people, their chewing, their vague nasalities.

The sound of apples torn by teeth, no matter
who the Eve, what snake, set your teeth on edge;
the horror of soup dripping back
into the plate—

this is why you left them. This
is what even the forest floor offered—
you now running feral, adopting the self—
silence as solace, so long longed for, so late.

3

"I think at times of women
anonymous of my past,
of sexual agonies
glazed by rain;
who were they, after all?
Some of us no longer believe
in things—when I
was a child I thought
the great shocking confession
was lack of faith in God
but it's things whose pale
emptiness most threatens:
their faces gone, their touch—
it was only spiritual,
after all:
I went among prostitutes;
no one, not preacher nor poet,
condemns a vice not his own.
Who among you can keep
faith in any way or thing?
He who still believes in stones
can throw the first one."

4

O the story is too absurd, too silly
To take more of our time. Who believes
In a boy become a famous composer,
Country born but soon given freely

To carouse and amply complain among
The famous and foolish of Paris?
He disappears, then stories are told
Of a wild man *à la campagne*, a song

On occasion being heard from some direction
He was last seen in; being in want
Of some Romantic story, the papers took it
Up for a time, then dropped it—wrecks on

Some barbaric coast, another war, took up
All available attention. Of course there was
The matter of the boy, the body, to dispose of;
He was simply lost, the funeral (you can look up

All this in your *Grove*), divinely operatic,
Was held for the sake of surface and appearance;
His mistress was a diva, now forgotten;
His mother, now dead, kept records in her attic.

5

Wretched excess. Soon our happy hearts will quiver,
they say, with a melody of peace. The emperor's
old clothes intrigued me as a boy; I wondered
who got them, what glass case was caused to hold
the old, the prefidelity relics. Pardon
was my fondest wish, faith my weakest link.
Hope seemed then the faith of scoundrels. . . .
I *hope* the emperor is not naked? But I knew
which virtue to count on: Charity.

Here was strength even a boy could understand
because a boy believes in the body. A boy lives there
like an athlete or dancer, except sometimes the pain
moves him out. Sometimes like a fire drill in the night
the pain makes him leave to stand outside and look,
thinking, Is that a tongue of flame,
is that me burning?

As for me, I need the memory of old men to keep
me whole. The thought that loss of life or limb
is mere manipulation, loosening the garment,
so to speak—a test of faith, not fate. And the true
saints are those tailors taking upon themselves the task
of turning us to transparence, that curious scandal.

Listen, you who are old enough to remember:
when Eichmann was tried in his glass booth,
did he *look* separate, apart from us?
Was there air in that box, the same as ours?

You know those international conferences,
when men and women in glass boxes talk into their fists,
their microphones, the simultaneous translators breathing
the air of Paris in New York, of Moscow in Chile?

Or the paintings of Francis Bacon, the red Pope
purifying in his square glass cage like Superman
changing clothes, shuffling his mortal coil
to emerge naked as an emperor talking
all languages, confessing to everything,
to every Jew and Gentile, dying like he meant it, naked.

About the author

Bin Ramke originally intended to be a mathematician; this book has been influenced by his earlier studies in the sciences. He is now director of the writing program and associate professor of English at the University of Denver; he is also editor of the Contemporary Poetry Series of the University of Georgia Press. He has taught at Columbus College, Georgia, and at the University of Georgia, and now teaches in the summer at the Aspen Writers' Conference.

Ramke has won a number of awards for his poetry, beginning in 1977 with the Yale Younger Poets' award (Richard Hugo's first selection in the series) for his book *The Difference between Night and Day*. He has received a Texas Institute of Arts and Letters award, a Kayden Award in Arts from the University of Colorado, and two Pushcart Prizes. His other books are *White Monkeys* and *The Language Student*.

Ramke is a graduate of Louisiana State University (B.A. 1970), the University of New Orleans (M.A. 1971), and Ohio University (Ph.D. 1975). His home is in Denver.

About the book

The Erotic Light of Gardens is set in Meridien, a typeface designed in 1957 by the Swiss typographer Adrian Frutiger. The book was composed on the Linotron 202 by Marathon Typography Service, Inc. of Durham, North Carolina. The design is by Kachergis Book Design of Pittsboro, North Carolina.